GNOCK! GNOCK! JOKES

BEANObooks
geddes & grosset

D0994140

Gnock! Gnock!

Who's there?

Ammonia.

Ammonia who?

Ammonia [I'm only a] little girl who can't reach the door bell.

Gnock! Gnock!

Who's there?

Ya.

Ya who?

YAHOO? Is there a party going on in there?

Gnock! Gnock!

Who's there?

Lettuce.

Lettuce who?

Lettuce out, it's cold in here!

Gnock! Gnock!
Who's there?
The Sultan.
The Sultan who?
The Sultan pepper.

Gnock! Gnock!

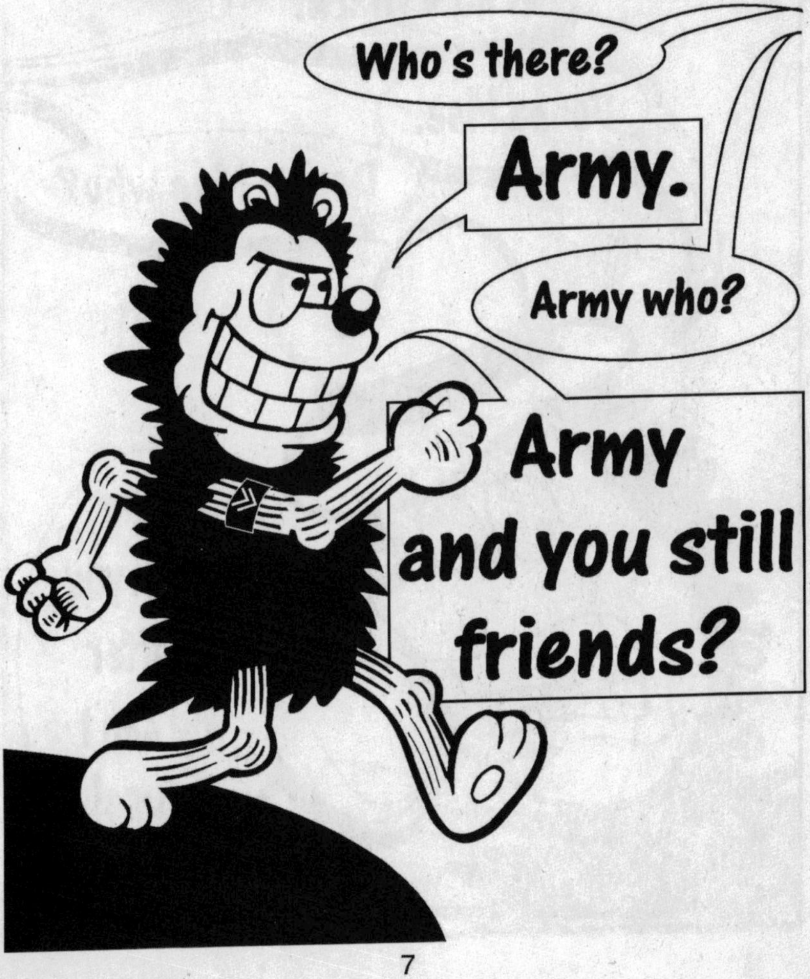

Gnock! Gnock!
Who's there?
Donna Mae.
Donna Mae who?
Donna Mae-k you an offer you can't refuse!

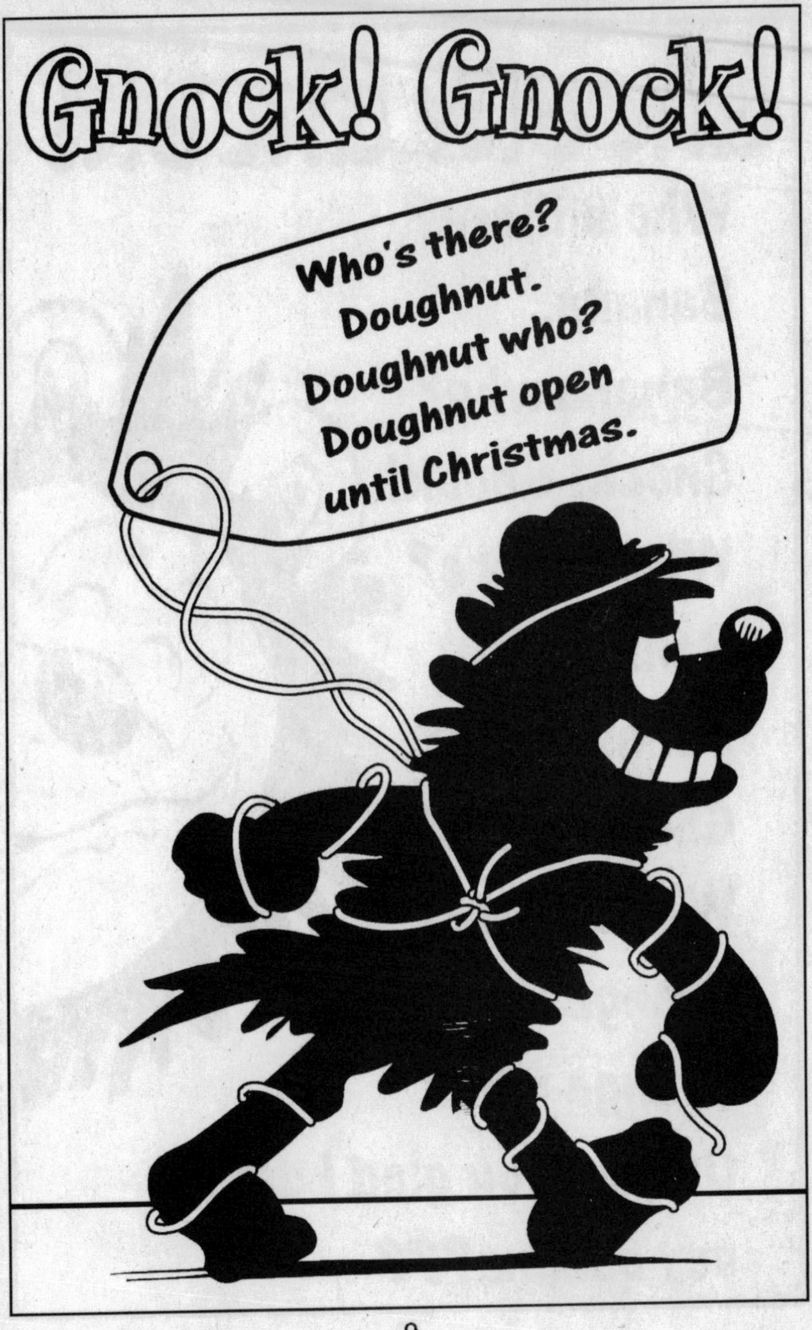

Gnock! Gnock!

Who's there?

Banana.

Banana who?

Gnock! Gnock!

Who's there?

Banana.

Banana who?

Gnock! Gnock!

Who's there?

Orange.

Orange who?

Orange you glad I didn't say banana???

Gnock! Gnock!

Who's there?

William.

William who?

William mind your own business?

Gnock! Gnock!

Who's there?

Boo.

Boo who?

Don't cry!

Gnock! Gnock!

Who's there?

Water.

Water who?

Water you, a gorilla?

Gnock! Gnock!

Who's there?

Wednesday.

Wednesday who?

Wednesday saints go marching in!

Gnock! Gnock!

Who's there?

Nobel.

Nobel who?

No bell so I'll Gnock.

Gnock! Gnock!

Who's there?

You.

You who?

Are you calling me?

Gnock! Gnock!

Who's there?

Cargo.

Cargo who?

Car go beep! beep!

beep! beep!

Gnock! Gnock!

Gnock! Gnock!

Who's there?
Police.
Police who?
Police open
the door.

Gnock! Gnock!

Who's there?

Dana.

Dana who?

Dana talk with your mouth full.

Gnock! Gnock!

Who's there?
Dotty.
Dotty who?
Dotty way the
cookie crumbles!

Gnock! Gnock!

Who's there?

Duane.

Duane who?

Duane the bath, I'm dwowning.

Gnock! Gnock!

Who's there?
Dragon.
Dragon who?
Dragon your feet again!

Gnock! Gnock!

Who's there?
Dummy.
Dummy who?
Dummy a favour and
go away.

Gnock! Gnock!

Who's there?
Willube.
Willube who?
Will you be
my valentine?

Gnock! Gnock!

Who's there?
Water.
Water who?
What are friends for!

Gnock! Gnock!

Who's there?

Disguise.

Disguise who?

Disguise the limit.

Gnock! Gnock!
Who's there?
Dawn.
Dawn who?
Dawn leave me out here in the cold.

Gnock! Gnock!

Who's there?

Deanna.

Deanna who?

Deanna-mals are restless, open the cage.

Who's there?

Daisy.

Daisy who?

Daisy plays, nights he sleeps.

Gnock! Gnock!

Who's there?
Disk.
Disk who?
Disk is a recorded message,
please leave your message
after the beep.

Gnock! Gnock!

Who's there?

Don Juan.

Don Juan who?

Don Juan to go to school today.

Gnock! Gnock!

Who's there?

Dennis.

Dennis who?

Dennis says I need to have a tooth out.

Gnock! Gnock!

Who's there?

Doctor.

Doctor who?

You just said it.

Gnock! Gnock!

Who's there?

Donald.

Donald who?

Donald come baby, cradle and all.

Gnock! Gnock!

Who's there?

Dinah.

Dinah who?
Dinah shoot
until you see
the whites of
their eyes.

Gnock! Gnock!

Who's there?
Darren.
Darren who?
Darren young man
in the flying machine.

Gnock! Gnock!

Who's there?

Diploma.

Diploma who?

Diploma to fix the leak.

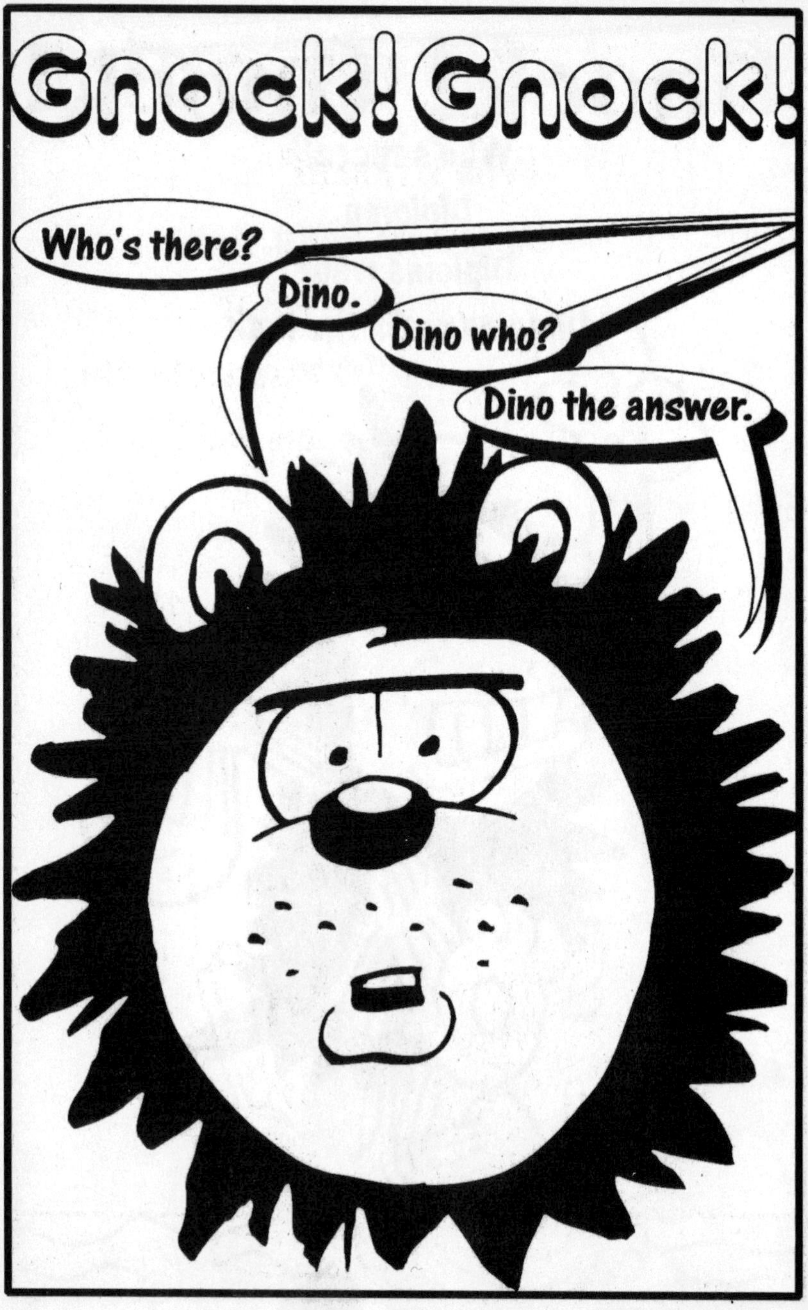
Gnock! Gnock!
Who's there?
Dino.
Dino who?
Dino the answer.

Gnock! Gnock!

Who's there?

Ice cream soda.

Ice cream soda who?

Ice cream soda neighbours wake up.

[I scream so the neighbours wake up.]

41

Gnock! Gnock!

Who's there?

Little old lady.

Little old lady who?

I didn't know you could yodel.

Gnock! Gnock!

Who's there?

Icon.

Icon who?

Icon tell you another joke. Do you want me to?

GNOCK!
GNOCK!

Who's there?
Joy.
Joy who?
Joil your roller
skates yesterday?

GNOCK! GNOCK!

Who's there?

Michael.

Michael who?

My collection of knock knock jokes is brilliant.

GNOCK! GNOCK!

Who's there?

Andy.

Andy who?

Andy knock knock jokes just keep on coming.

GNOCK! GNOCK!

Who's there?

Rufus.

Rufus who?

Rufus get a hole in it, carpet's getting wet.

GNOCK! GNOCK!

Who's there?
Ralph.
Ralph who?
Ralphabet goes from A-Z.

GNOCK! GNOCK!

Who's there?
Ivy.
Ivy who?
Ivish you vell.

GNOCK! GNOCK!

Who's there?
Ken.
Ken who?
Ken't you recognise my voice?

GNOCK!
GNOCK!

Who's there?

Liz.

Liz who?

Liz is getting ridiculous.

GNOCK! GNOCK!

GNOCK! GNOCK!

Who's there?
Francis.
Francis who?
France is next door
to Spain.

GNOCK! GNOCK!

Who's there?
Jeff.
Jeff who?
J-effer hear this joke before?

GNOCK! GNOCK!

Who's there?
Janet.
Janet who?
Janetor from the school.

GNOCK! GNOCK!

Who's there?
Hugo.
Hugo who?
Hugo away from this door now.

GNOCK!
GNOCK!

Who's there?

Joan.

Joan who?

Joan this old place?

GNOCK! GNOCK!

Who's there?
Judy.
Judy who?
Judeliver milk in
the mornings?

GNOCK! GNOCK!

Who's there?
Dougal.
Dougal who?
Do gulls live near the sea?

GNOCK! GNOCK!

Who's there?
Carmen.
Carmen who?
Carmen to the garden, Maude.

GNOCK! GNOCK!

Who's there?
Claire.
Claire who?
Claire to see you don't know.

GNOCK! GNOCK!

Who's there?
Thor.
Thor who?
Thort you'd ask me that.

GNOCK! GNOCK!

Who's there?

Petula.

Petula who?

Petulaugh at this gag.

GNOCK! GNOCK!

Who's there?
Aladdin.
Aladdin who?
Aladdin the rain.
Let me in.

GNOCK! GNOCK!

Who's there?
Jonah.
Jonah who?
Jonah doorbell?

GNOCK! GNOCK!

Who's there?
Saul.
Saul who?
Saul I'm going to tell you.

GNOCK! GNOCK!

Who's there?
Mister.
Mister who?
Mister window and knocked
on 'er door.

GNOCK! GNOCK!

Who's there?

Peg.

Peg who?

Peg your pardon, wrong door.

Gnock! Gnock!
Who's there?
Dime.
Dime who?
Dime to tell another Gnock! Gnock! joke.

Gnock! Gnock!
Who's there?
Radio.
Radio who?
Radio not, here I come!

Gnock! Gnock!

Who's there?

Alaska.

Alaska who?

Alaska one more time...let me in!

Gnock! Gnock!

Who's there?

I used.

I used who?

I used to be able to
reach the doorbell,
but now I can't.

Gnock! Gnock!

Who's there?
Toodle.
Toodle who?
Toodle-oo to you, too.

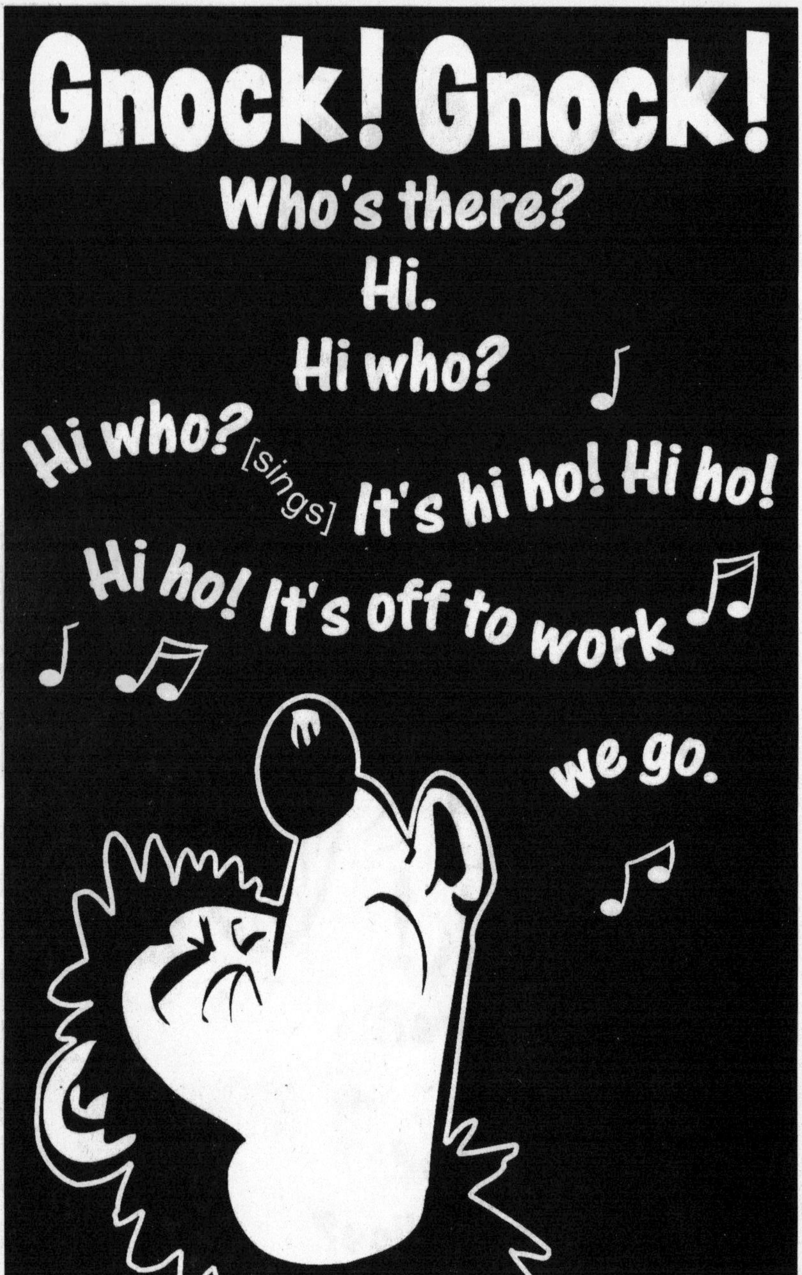

Gnock! Gnock!

Who's there?

House.

House who?

House it going?

Gnock! Gnock!

Who's there?

Canoe.

Canoe who?

Canoe come out
to play?

Gnock! Gnock!
Who's there?
Dona.
Dona who?
Dona sit under the apple tree
with anyone but me.

Cnock! Cnock!

Who's there?
Waiter.
Waiter who?
Waiter a minute while I tie my shoe.

Bones
Bones
Bo

GNOCK! GNOCK!

Who's there?
Ewan.
Ewan who?
Ewan me are in a knock knock joke.

GNOCK! GNOCK!

Who's there?
Howard.
Howard who?
Howard is it raining out here?

GNOCK! GNOCK!
Who's there?
Murry.
Murry who?
Murry Christmas,
Happy New Year.

GNOCK! GNOCK!

Who's there?
Franz
Franz who?
Franz is just across the channel.